POET TREE IN MOTION

Royal Shepherd

Introduction

In 1985 I picked up a book by the Author: Langston Hughes, and read a piece called "Dress Up". That poem opened my eyes to the world of poetry. Ever since then, I have impressed my words on anyone who would listen. Now, it's 31 years later, and with this book "Poet Tree In Motion" I hope to follow in the footsteps of all the great poets, by opening the eyes of readers all around, to this wonderful world of poetry!

Book Description

This is a book of literature, filled with inspirational and encouraging poems, that will enlighten the reader to see life in a whole new light.

Contents

Introduction _____ 2
Book Description _____ 4
Chapter 1 _____ 9
   WORD PLAY _____ 9
   Tears of The Righteous _____ 11
   PICTURE THAT _____ 12
   WHEN I WAS WEAK _____ 13
   MY PRAYER _____ 14
   I JUST WANT TO THANK GOD _____ 15
   ENERGY _____ 16
   THE QUESTION IS? _____ 17
   Wait On the Lord _____ 18
   When The Saints Go Marching In _____ 19
   THEY JUST CAN'T SEE THE BEAUTY IN ME _____ 20
   MANNING UP STANDING UP _____ 21
   THROUGH GODS EYES _____ 22
   WE ARE SOLDIER'S _____ 23
   IT'S AN ALL OUT STRUGGLE _____ 24
   DIVINE FAVOR _____ 25
   ONE OF THE ONES _____ 26
   HAND ME THE CROSS!! _____ 27
   IDENTIFIED _____ 28
   I'M ON ASSIGNMENT _____ 29

THAT PARADISE	30
CHAPTER TWO	*31*
I AM PEACE	31
SPECIAL DELIVERY!	33
MY MISTRESS	34
ENDLESS PURSUIT	35
HOW I LOVE YOU	36
I KNOW AT TIMES	37
I Believe In Love	38
MY GIRL	39
A LETTER OF LOVE	40
SPECIAL FRIENDS	41
TRUE BEAUTY	42
"YOU'RE THE LOVE OF MY LIFE"	43
LOVE	44
BEAUTY IS HER NAME	45
WHOLE HEARTEDLY	46
CLOSER	47
I DID IT FOR YOU	48
KISS ON THE CHEEK	49
LOVE IS A CRAZY GAME	50
PRESENCE FROM THE WINDOW	51
CHAPTER THREE	*52*
LET MY PEOPLE GO	52
I DON'T BELIEVE	54

I'M RUNNING OUT OF TIME!	55
AM I MY BROTHER'S KEEPER	56
SERIOUSLY FOR REAL	57
WHAT ARE WE DOING HERE?	58
HOW COULD I?	59
DEAF AND BLIND	60
YOU NEVER KNOW	61
DON'T PLAY THE PART OF A LOSER!	62
DANGEROUS MINDS	63
HAND OUTS	64
SAVE YOURSELF	65
OPINIONS	66
ANGER	67
CHAPTER FOUR	68
ONE BAD NIGHT	68
MEN OF HONOR	69
HOLD ON	70
I JUST WANT TO BE	71
DON'T DROP THE BALL	72
THE MORE YOU GROW	73
OPPORTUNITY	74
NEVER STOP TRYING	75
I HAVE SEEN THAT FACE BEFORE	76
I'M GOING ALL THE WAY!	77
EXPRESSION	78
EVERYTHING IS GONNA BE ALRIGHT!	79

CHAPTER FIVE	*80*
BACK IN THE OLD DAYS !	80
THE CITY OF POETRY	81
MAYBE IT'S A SLOW LEAK	82
I'M JUST TAKING IT EASY	83
A NEW YEAR	84
IN THE MORNING	85
I KNOW IT'S REAL	86
THAT'S MOMMA'S LIL MAN	87
Chapter SIX	*88*
"Quotes"	88
Special Shout Outs to:	95
About The Author	97
Inspirational Songs	98

Chapter 1

WORD PLAY

In the beginning, it was the word, and the word was with GOD, and the word was GOD, see, God was so precise, and persistent, he spoke his self into existence. That's why I use this speech, when I teach, when I preach, I try to reach, my hand down to the weak, I'm strong but I'm meek. But my spirit has sprung a leak, and it's pouring out verbally, but I can remember, when words were just words to me. Now I feel, that nouns and verbs, deserves to be, bowed down to, saluted, patronized polluted. To every nation and every country, from Haiti to Hungry, from Monday to Sunday to Mandela and Gundy. Ain't life funny, I never expected that my metaphors and assemblies, would be used as tools to set my people free. I knew about Moses and Martin Luther King. But I was so enthused with money and numbers I didn't think words could add up to anything, so I started checking out the word, to see what the word was saying. And I heard, stand up and stop playing, be courageous and daring, be patient but preparing, to show kindness, and caring. What kind of words are you sharing? Are you tearing folks down, or you building them up, are you emptying them out, or you filling their cup? Cause life is to short, to keep your tail tucked, we need to instruct and inspire, enlighten, and admire, every word, that was heard, from the flood to the fire, be live like a wire, and always reach higher, put your pride aside, then you can call God Sire, Now let the words that you say, be the words that you pray. And if you let God pave the way, you can save the whole day! That's just A little word play!

Tears of The Righteous

Tears of the righteous, they might just, fill the whole land, or heal an old man, or shield my soul when, my family is starring down on me saying. "Please no! don't go"! But I'll be already gone, it was my time to move on, this old world has held me down for so long. That's why my biggest prayer to God, is for peace of mind, and that I find that peace in time, to help me increase from being least in line, see I don't want to be late, for heavens gates, and God says, there's no more space, you took to long to find your faith, That's why we need the tears of the righteous, cause they might just, fill the whole land, or heal an old man, then conceal my soul than, wash away my worries and doubts, and fill me up with that faith, that Jesus was talking about. See I'm not a righteous man and I don't claim to be, but I found out how to get into heaven, and I want to sneak Y'all in there with me. First of all, God gave Jesus the keys, but the key hole, is so low, you have to get on your knees with Jesus, to ever get in that door. That's why we need the tears of the righteous, cause they might just, fill the whole land, or heal an old man, or put you together and give you a master plan, that's the tears of the righteous! Amen!

PICTURE THAT

God has painted us a picture, and it's perfect, and it's worth it, we're just waiting on the negatives to surface, we did good, we deserve it, but when we first started, we were kind of nervous, we didn't have a job, we were out of service, I guess that's what stirred up all the worries, now let me paint you a picture of this story, picture this, a boy growing up and he's all alone, his father is on drugs, and his mother is always gone, she has a lil boyfriend, so she's barely at home, he's left to fin for his self, he has to make it on his own, since his dad was stuck on rocks, he decided, to throw the first stone, a few thousand dollars later, this lil boy was grown, he bought new clothes, and a fancy car, the best of everything, like he was a superstar, then he started smoking weed and sipping bar, I guess that's why his drug dealing career didn't make it very far, one night he fell asleep at the light, and got pulled over by the law, I guess he never thought, he would get stopped by cops, cause he had a pocket full of cash, and a stash, full of rocks, while on lock, he found his self all alone again, so he started reading the bible, and found God in the pin, and we he got out, God was all he talked about, he was really changed, he got serious about life, and he stop playing games, God became his father, and the church became his mother, and since Jesus Christ saved his life, he became his brother, even though everything in his past life was gone, with this new family he new he would never have to be alone, PICTURE THAT!

POET TREE IN MOTION   ROYAL SHEPHERD

WHEN I WAS WEAK

When I thought I was strong, I found out I was weak, because when I fell to the street, I could smell the defeat, I just shook my head, and said, "How did I ever get beat", But I knew exactly what it was, God had took his favor away from me, So, for a while, I wallowed around in self pity, tell I finally decided to ask God to forgive me, for all my sins, and I knew right then, that I would never fight again, I guess it takes a heck of a lost, to pay the cost, for a heck of a lot of wins, and that's how that chapter ends, And this is where this new chapter in my life begins, when I thought I was weak God made me strong, he whispered some words to me, then I wrote them in a song, precept upon precept, line upon line, God gave me his power, and he made me divine, and the root, of a poetry branch that would bare much fruit, by not being afraid to tell people the truth, because it's the truth that sets us free, and gives us an option to make our own decisions, and a opportunity, to become what ever we want to be, it was God that gave these words to me, and the courage to enlighten your eyes to see, that at first I was weak, but now I am strong, because of the power of Christ that rest upon me!

MY PRAYER

God please forgive me for my sins, an lead me to a path of peace, when my days come to an end, An while I'm praying, help me to understand, the plans that you have for me as a man, put in me the faith to know I can, and the strength to fulfill your will, to enlighten and instill, let me be filled with the faith, to move mountain's and split seas, and please teach me your ways, so my soul shall be at ease, you already know the plans that you have for me, to have peace and love and prosperity, so give me the eyes to see, and the ears to hear, the words you have for me, direct my feet, in the path where I need to be, so I can provide for my family, and keep us strong, teach me what to teach them, so we can all just get along, cause it's not easy trying to make it on our own, without you God we always seem to go wrong, I want to thank you God for every blessing that you bring, and I ask all of this in Jesus name! Amen!

POET TREE IN MOTION   ROYAL SHEPHERD

I JUST WANT TO THANK GOD

I just want to thank God for the ability, to write and recite, this poetry, I appreciate this gift that he's giving me, because I have changed the way I use to be, And usually, when God makes a man stop playing, he has plans for that man, if it's in his will, then I can, and I will understand, every mistake that I make, and every word that he's saying, I'm constantly praying that he leads the way, and guides my feet so I won't go astray, I find comfort in his holy arms, and I hope he knows I adore him, And hopefully one day I can show him, that the words that he's giving me has set me free, and maybe just maybe, I will become the man, that he made me to be, So I just want to thank God for the blessings, for teaching me these lessons, the one on one session, and the late night confessions, Because I know all that it takes, is one slip up, one mistake, A little lack of faith, that's all that it takes, to put me in last place, And make me lose the whole race, That's why I just want to thank God for all his mercy and his grace!

ENERGY

I had to learn how to channel my energy, because I almost let the enemy, enter me, but I knew that would be the end of me, so I got on my bended knee, and I said a prayer to G.O.D, because I knew somehow he would set me free, and let me see, the place where I was, and the place where I needed to be, I was lost and blind, and just could not see, Then I heard a voice say to me, Son, I can save your soul, But you have to catch your snap, because you are out of control, Your patients is short, and your heart is cold, So you must humble yourself in order to grow, See I sit high, and I look low, so I know you are not doing the things, that I sent you there for, So I said 'My father who art in heaven, please forgive me for my sins, is it any kind of way, that I might make amends, Because I lost my way, trying to make some ends, God, I will give you full control, just please make me whole again, And I knew right then, that I had been changed, thru all the hurt and pain, my time had finally came, And God had changed, the channels to my energy, so I no longer had to worry about the enemy, trying to enter me, Because God alone, only knows when the end will be!

THE QUESTION IS?

  I'm just a spirit passing, on fire, full of passion, and the question that I'm asking, is, are you able, strong and stable, and ready to change your life, so you can eat at the Lord's table, to taste of the body, and the blood, What are you willing to sacrifice, for it, are you willing to lay down your life, deny your flesh and start doing what's right, despite the struggle, we have to win the fight, But I'm just a spirit passing, on fire, full of passion, and the question that I ask is, are you still living in the past, still moving to fast, unable to grasp, an everyday task, if you are, than that's bad, you need to get your spirit in order, because if not, things will just get harder and harder, tell you start to, lose focus, and get side tracked, by that cankerworm, that locus, because he sets up stumbling blocks that can choke us, But see me, I don't have time to play, so I'm not listening, to nothing that the devil is trying to say, Cause I'm just a spirit passing, on fire, full of passion, and the question that I'm asking is, are you pure, and are you sure, and ready to endure, the persecution, the slander, do you think this is something that you're strong enough to handle, Because God is about to send you out as a light, so he will be able to judge right, because the people that hate you, have the same spirit, of those who crucified Christ, Then you will become, just a spirit passing, on fire, full of passion, But this new life you will be living, will be everlasting!

Wait On the Lord

If you find yourself being approached by a stumbling block don't loose faith, take a seat and wait, wait on the Lord, he knows the Devils tricks and he Ain't falling for it. Even Jesus was tempted for forty days by the enemy, right after he was baptized and anointed to go on with his ministry, God presence shined down like a radiant dove, and he said this is my beloved son that I am well pleased of. See that's when Satan start hating, and tries to accuse you, he will use all his tools to try and confuse you. He will lie and cheat, and make his tricks look like treats, That's who places that stumbling block at your feet. But don't loose faith, take a seat and wait, wait on the Lord, he knows the Devil's tricks and he's not falling for it!

POET TREE IN MOTION   ROYAL SHEPHERD

When The Saints Go Marching In

I'm just somebody, that believes, that somebody could be the best, I said some prayers, and some poems, and I let God do the rest. Even though I went through some test, faith was my friend, that help me to excel, and prevail through the end, and I still go thru things, every now and then, Sometime I get rattled, with this battle with sin, And at times I fall down , but I get back up again, Cause I refuse to loose, I was born to win, And I got to be in that number, when the saint go marching in, Oh when the saints, go marching in, oh when the saints go marching in, oh how I want to be, In that number, when the saints go marching in, I believe I would just die, if I was stuck on the side line, as the saints pass me by, That's why I try, and I try, and God knows that's no lie, I'm going to hold up blood stained banner until I die, He lift me up with his unchanging hands and he enhanced, my plans, and made my plans advance ,and I'm just an old sinner, he gave a second chance!

THEY JUST CAN'T SEE THE BEAUTY IN ME

They just can't see the beauty in me because they just don't know my God , My God ,They just can't see the Jesus in me because they just don't know my heart my heart, In order to see me at my best you had to see me at my worst, My life started off like a curse or a country song verse, But like good wine in due time , God made me divine ,Set apart, one of a kind, I still remember when temptation had me blind ,had me bind, Then God came along and put my odds and ends in line, dust me off and gave me this brand new awesome shine, This glow and now I know, what I was sent here for, And I don't have to walk around lost in the dark no more , THEY JUST CAN'T SEE THE BEAUTY IN ME " Some people still don't understand how God defines the beauty in a man, They obtain their bachelor's and master's, but still don't know the master plan, So when I pray I ask God in my prayers, to always here me, and stay near me, and let the faith of my people fall weary, I know this might sound hard, but it's going to be some eyes that can't see and ears that can't hear the lord, The ones that can see it still won't know they saw it, THEY JUST CAN'T SEE THE BEAUTY IN ME BECAUSE THEY JUST DON'T KNOW MY GOD, THEY JUST CAN'T SEE THE JESUS IN ME, BECAUSE THEY JUST DON'T KNOW MY HEART!

MANNING UP STANDING UP

I'm manning up standing up whole heartedly, By giving God every part of me, because I'm starting to see that's how it ought to be, Mind body and soul, just let the spirit take control, While reaching for my goals, so I can grow, Just looking at my life trying to take things slow, cause I know, if I get to moving to fast, My pleasure turns to pain, and my treasure turn to trash, so I'm going to keep my eyes on the task at hand, and that's building myself up ,so I can be a better man, make me some plans, and goals, plant me some seeds in some souls, I'm going to build um up fill um up, with everything I got, It's the spirit of God that make me so hot, The way I walk the way I talk the way I praise his name, Thru the poetry that lives in me, and every song I sing, and it didn't happen all in one night, I had to pray and have faith, steady meditate, and wait, for things to go right, but now I know that I'm blessed, it was all a process, that made me progress, and have this success, you can't just, sit back and settle for less, You have to be determine, always learning when it's concerning God, because he gave you life, by sending his son, down here to die for it, that's why I speak like I speak, and preach like I preach, Because I have faith that someday somebody will be reached, that's why I'm manning, up standing up, whole heartily, because I'm starting to see, that's how it ought to be, mind body and soul just let the spirit take control!

THROUGH GODS EYES

Through Gods eyes, I can see the beauty that's in you, you have become perfect in Gods sight, by the things you've been through, the scratches and the scars, and the bruises, from trials and tribulations, these are the qualifications that he uses, so don't get confused by your newness, because the transformation, that's transpiring, only God can do this, to change you into a bran new creation, he breaks you down, then builds you up, so you will be able to restore nations, congratulations , You are a new member to the team, through Gods eyes, this is what I've seen, You will obtain the gift of prophesy, and will be able to discern dreams, Do you know what this means, your one of the ones, Sanctified, and set aside, you're one of God's sons, You'll be sent out, to seek and save, which was lost, and you will be covered by the blood that was shed on the cross, Jesus paid the cost, And he paved the way, For us to inherit this eternal life that we live today, Because thru God's eyes you're spectacular, immaculate, supreme, If you could've only seen what God saw thru my eyes in you, you would know exactly what I mean!

WE ARE SOLDIER'S

We are soldiers, in the army, we have to fight, all though we have to die, we have to hold up, the blood stained banner, we have to hold it up, until we die, God didn't create us to live a life of sorrow, he had plans that men would lend and not borrow, and create a better day tomorrow, So since he has so much hope in me, I will try to see clearly, so I can be the best that I can be, And more, than I'll be pure, and sure, that I can endure, whatever comes my way, Then I'll be able to prepare paths and ways, and teach people to praise, I might, possibly be the light, for folks to see right, so they can walk into there brighter days, Because we are soldiers on the battle field, That knows that God is real, and that prayers do heal, we have the protected seal, we were built to build, God established us from birth, made us from dirt, so he knows our worth, we were sent to help and not hurt, To exert our blessings, teach lessons, to help with progressing, Constantly comforting those with confessions, Plant seeds, and watch them grow, let the people know, that they reap what they sow, We have to be a people that people can admire, A people, that's trust worthy, because people don't trust a liar, and only the enemy lies, And we don't want to become a people that people despise, Because we are soldiers on the rise, trying to save some people's lives, By opening up there eyes, to the lord Jesus Christ, The only true way to eternal life, The lord is the blood sacrifice, For sin, he lived then he died, and was raised again, So who so ever, shall call on his name shall be saved from sin, WE ARE SOLDIERS, IN THE ARMY, WE HAVE TO FIGHT, ALL THOUGH WE HAVE TO DIE   WE HAVE TO HOLD UP, THE BLOOD STAINED BANNER, WE HAVE TO HOLD IT UP UNTIL WE DIE!

IT'S AN ALL OUT STRUGGLE

It's an all out struggle, that's my lil saying, But a friend of mines told me, when you find Christ you don't have to struggle no more, But through my experience in life I found out that wasn't true though, Me and everybody I see, when we came to Christ I saw our struggle's grow, We struggled with change, struggled with pain, just simply struggling to maintain, finding Christ is not just paradise, people still struggle with all kind of things, And people think I have it easy, but they don't want to do what I had to do, are go thru, what I went thru, And I know they don't want to be where I've been, incarcerated, locked down in the pen, doing time for my crime, paying my price for sin, No I'm not ashamed to tell you where I've been, or where I'm going, because the time that I lost, gave me the strength to show the love that I'm showing, and to plant these seeds that I've been growing, See I'm spoiled by God, his love has a satisfaction guarantee, he made a covenant with me, That he would supply my every need, But even through all the blessings and mercy that God shows, Just battling with my flesh lets me know, that it's still an all out struggle though, See I'm not the first one to struggle and I'm almost sure I won't be the last, God left those scripture's in the bible, to let us know that folks struggled in the past, So when you come across these situation and circumstances in your life, Don't try to do it on your own, all alone, God gave us his son Jesus Christ to turn those stumbling blocks into stepping stones, Scripture says, "WHEN I WAS A CHILD I WALKED LIKE A CHILD I THOUGHT LIKE A CHILD, I PLAYED CHILDISH GAMES", See I struggled then and I struggle now, but I can see how much I've changed, Now in everything I do, and in everything I say, I put God first, in every verse, I pray, God please forgive me for my sins, I know it's an all out struggle but I'm fighting to win!

POET TREE IN MOTION ROYAL SHEPHERD

DIVINE FAVOR

I'm walking this tight line, hoping that I might fine, Divine favor in the Lord, I've been trying but it's hard, So I decided to start to meditate, So maybe somehow I could relate to God, Right then and there I saw it, in A dream, God was showing me what divine favor really means, It starts with his grace and mercy, with unmerited favor, that means we're not even worthy, yea, you heard me, God wants us to be blessed above measure, He has us set apart in his heart, as his own living treasure, We are God's ministry, Folks like you and me, That uses the spirit of the Lord to help people see, That if they walk by faith, and not by sight, The Lord our God will be your light, and everything will be alright, No we don't fight against flesh and blood, But the power of the Lord has prepared us for it, Prepared us for victory, So when I'm not doing my job he keeps convicting me, All in my soul, when I start playing games, he helps me regain control, he makes me whole, and lets me know, That I am an Ambassador, his divine diplomat, one of a kind, A sworn soldier of Royal design, Crowned with Honor and Glory, I was made DIVINE!

ONE OF THE ONES

I'm one of the ones, But I'm not in the NFL, NFC, or the NBA, I'm one of the ones, that get on my knees and pray, And say the things that God needs me to say, I'm not saying that some times I don't go astray, Because I drop the ball almost every day, But I pick it right up and I go for the goal, I keep my mind on God, because I know that he's in control, This weekend, God used me to anoint one of my podna's to be a deacon, And it's a good thing to know that God is using you, It's a tremendous change, from the things I use to do, And I'm pretty sure he can use you too, If you just let go of your past, he will make all things new, That's why I'm one of the ones, that's precious in his sight, He brought me out of darkness, so I could shed a little light, now I'm marvelous, And glad that God has let me be apart of this, Life long mission, by opening people's eyes, and helping them get in position, First they start with a little suspicion, then that leads to all kinds of crazy superstition, Then God puts me in the mix, to let them see what they've been missing, And I will give them the real, If their willing to listen, Because I'm not feeding them fish, I'm taking them fishing! Because I'm one of the ones!

HAND ME THE CROSS!!

IF it's my time, then hand me the cross, so I can carry it, but God please give me the courage like Harriot, Malcolm and Martin! Cause I see this new generation has already started, split seas of poverty, that has been parted,! People manning up standing up, whole hearted. Reaching out, speaking out, reminding folks, what the struggle was all about, fighting for freedom and equality, in the American way, freedom of speech, freedom to teach, freedom to get on our knees and pray! So what more can I say? But hand me the cross! Because I see how much can be gained, from one mans loss, some even paid the cost, with their own blood, if it were possible for your death to redeem my life, would you pay for it? No! You probably wouldn't! And that's not what I'm asking at all, just if you have a friend in need, Answer the phone when they call! What's wrong with Y'all! JESUS died for our sins, so we should at least, humble ourselves and try to help our friends! that's why I'm here tonight, so I can shed A little light, so hand me the cross, or hand me the mic, hand me A pen, then I'm going to sit here and write, how the death of JESUS CHRIST, has gave us this life, so it's my right, and my job, to help, JESUS said " love GOD, with all your heart, and love your neighbor, like you love yourself! See I probably won't ever save the world, or set a nation free! But I can help A hungry family, that's living next door to me! So hand me the cross!

IDENTIFIED

When I was identified, as being sanctified, Satan tried his best, To confuse me, and misuse me, and put me to the test, But I knew that I was blessed, and that I possessed, God's favor, because he sent his only son to die for my sins, and become my savior, that's why I speak boldly, with confidence, because God told me, that I was heaven sent, so ever since, I'm never tense, because I know my salvation is secure, so now I'm walking in authority, because his blood has made me pure, but it's an urgency, an emergency, that I stand to be a witness, I talk the talk, Because I walk the walk, when it comes to being about my father's business, each decision that I make, is weighed up properly, I have the power of prophecy, because I am God's property, I can speak in tongue and bring the dead back to life, wake up and rise, you're alive, in the name of Jesus Christ, But I have a vital message that I must share, and you really need to hearken, I am not the only person, that God has called to be working, it's a lot of people that need to be saved, and some changes that need to be made, for certain, you see the folks they are hurting, while you look at them like a burden, they keep knocking at your door, but you keep sneaking and peaking, thru your curtain, But you know what would really be a shame, if you make it all the way to heaven, and God says, he's never known your name, and you haven't bared any fruit, just toss him in the flames, So don't get identified, as being sanctified, and not really doing your best, cause Satan will confuse you and misuse you and you might just fell the test!

POET TREE IN MOTION   ROYAL SHEPHERD

I'M ON ASSIGNMENT

See I'm on assignment, and I'm just trying, to fulfill God's will, no matter what the world may feel, I must try my best to reveal what is real, but I must keep this message concealed, until my people has changed just a lil, bowed down and kneeled, tell their heart starts to heal, and then their character can be build, with passion and zeal, and that change can establish and maintain, a relationship with God, that will always sustain, that can help them thru the pain, my message is plain, the only reason I came, is because I'm on a mission from God, he said he had something to show me and I saw it, it was life and it was hard, I saw people's ego's get scarred, money get short, people losing heart, I even seen some who's whole life fell apart, God showed me all kinds of signs, thru these old eyes of mines, when I think about it, sometimes I start crying, but still trying, to understand, the value of a man, I don't fully know God's master plan, but I play my part, as a helping hand, I can't do much, but I do as much as I can, And I can still here God saying, son of man, what do you see, I see some people that's locked up, that need to be free, and I see some people that are free, but they are locked up spiritually, under the devil's confinement, I came to tell you, let go and let God this is my assignment!

THAT PARADISE

Take them to that paradise, show them what it's looking like, Tell them about Jesus Christ, that he is a living sacrifice, For our life, he paid the ultimate price, and thru his blood, he made it right, I guess that's why, he's the light, cause that night, he paved the way, That's why it's his name we pray, Hosanna to the son of David, We praise his name because it's sacred, And it's blessed, Righteous and just, and I know that this doesn't sound hard, But it has to come from the heart, God's not excepting anything short, First off, you must start, to believe in Jesus Christ, And know that thru his death, he gave you life, That's the beginning of paradise!

CHAPTER TWO

I AM PEACE

The other day I saw something so crazy, One of my podna's hugged up with one of our other podna's old lady, See to me that's so shady, It's just not real, That's the kind of thing that be getting folks killed, We been knowing dude since we were lil, and that's how you feel, We all went to the same elementary, Now you have me looking at you like if that were my girl, you would do the same thing to me, And you know they have been together forever, like he raised her, Then they get in a lil argument, now you have her in your arms trying to save her, And in your eyes you think it's right, And I will be willing to bet that you have plans on sleeping with her tonight, But in actuality, that's wrong, that's what I'm trying to get you to see, You're coveting another man's wife, about to commit adultery, See I am peace, I'm love, I'm fashion, I'm passion, I'm all of the above, I'm a kiss I'm a hug, I'm the hole you done dug, You like it when I talk nicely but you don't like when I shoot slugs, Hey, What's going on lil brother, I haven't seen you in a while, I heard you got married, and Congratulations, on your new child, I see you're still clean, you know I always loved your style, But I heard, from a lil bird, that you've been living kind of foul, You know I never been the one to gossip, or beat around the bush, And anytime you ever needed me I gave you that extra push, Here it is, I heard you've been cheating, and beating on your wife, You're like my lil brother, I've known you all your life, And that's not how you were raised, your momma raised you right, Just hear me out and listen, I'm just trying to tell you the truth to give you an option to make your own decision, And no matter what, I will always love you, better than any brother can, But I have to tell you lil bro, you have a family now it's time to stop playing, You are not a boy anymore it's time to be a man, I am peace I'm love, I'm fashion, I'm passion, I'm all of the above, I'm a kiss, I'm a hug, I'm the hole you done dug, you like it when I talk nicely, but you don't like it when I shoot slugs!

SPECIAL DELIVERY!

      God gave me someone with a special heart, one of a kind and set apart, a master piece, a work of art, A candle in the dark, a fun place in the park, Someone who always has my back and keeps me on track, God I need you to please send me someone like that, I know beauty is a must, one that doesn't fuss, And someone I will be able to trust, A love with no measure, my own hidden treasure, that fills me with pleasure, Someone I can shape and mole, that has a heart of gold, Somebody soft to hold, that can keep me warm when my nights are cold, So when I get nice and old, I can look back and see how much we have grown together, And she will tell me, Baby we are not old, we are just getting better, God I don't ask for much, But I need you to do this one thing for me, send me the perfect love right away, SPECIAL DELIVERY!

MY MISTRESS

I'm just standing here, staring at my mistress, Thinking how beautiful she looks in this dress, but wondering how did I ever get myself in this mess, I have a gorgeous wife at home, that I love, And this beautiful woman that I'm with, that I'm always thinking of, I'm in the best and worst place I've ever been in my life, stuck between a rock and a hard spot, with my mistress, and my wife, this was never how I planned it, to go off and leave my family abandoned, I must have just panicked, Maybe when things got hard, I just took things for granite, and when I think of it now, I still can't under stand it, but I do know, that I felt like I was stranded and stuck, Shipwreck and shit out of luck, and I don't have any place to pass the buck, far as I know, my wife hasn't done anything wrong, she cooks, she cleans, goes to work, then she comes back home, we share the same house, and she doesn't even know I'm gone, the only time we talk, is when she calls me on the phone, I must have a heart of stone, to go and just leave my wife alone, I'm in the best and the worst place I ever been in my life stuck between a rock and a hard place with my mistress and wife, my mistress knows about my wife, but my wife doesn't have a clue, and I don't think she could ever understand, what I'm really going thru, But I try to keep it real, I check in from time to time, and I pay all the bills, and I know it's not right, but I like how it feels, my wife could never find out, I would probably drown in her tears, right now this is my greatest fear, while I'm just standing here, staring at my mistress, thinking how beautiful she looks, in this dress, then out of the blue, you know who appears, I'm in the best and worst place I've ever been in my life, stuck between a rock and a hard spot with my mistress and my wife!

POET TREE IN MOTION ROYAL SHEPHERD

ENDLESS PURSUIT

See I'm on an endless pursuit of happiness, And just so happen this, morning I met a chick so gorgeous, I guess God just, wanted me to meet her, a beautiful blond hair senorita, so I decided to greet her, I said Bueno Dias senorita, and in a broken lingo she said "Ello, can you tell me how to get to south main", and before I could get a chance to explain, my baby mamma came, talking about, oh this your new thing, I said "if it was, what does it matter to you, we're not together "and she said, "we probably would be, if you knew how to treat women better", I said, "I know how to treat women just fine, I just got sick and tired of your old silly behind, she said, "Yeah right, you didn't say that last night", I said, "I didn't even see you last night, you see how you're so crazy", I wouldn't even be talking to you if it wasn't for our baby, you dead wrong, then I looked around and my little senorita was gone, I jumped in the truck and went on home, I had to get some rest, if I was still going out later on, see I'm on an endless pursuit of happiness, and just so happen this, evening, on the way to do some poetry, at the corner of main, guess who I see, my little senorita, in the car next to me, She smiled and I melted, then she blew me a kiss, and I felt it, that cut the deck, so I dealt it, just so happen this, was the end of my endless pursuit of happiness!

HOW I LOVE YOU

I want to whisper in your ear, I love you, a thousand times, So you can get a brief idea, of how your love stays on my mind, You're like music to me, a sweet melody, that makes my life complete, a treat, and the rhythm to my heart beat, I promise you a life time of pleasure, love with no measure, I'll start by giving you my heart as your own hidden treasure, you are everything that I need, Because you give me life, like the air that I breathe, Oh how I love you, you're a tasty delight, pure pleasure to my sight, perfection at it's peek, God made you just right, You're erotic, and hypnotic, you keep me in a trance, I want to be under your command, every chance that I can, You're my woman and I am your man, but I'm still your number one fan, How I love you!

POET TREE IN MOTION   ROYAL SHEPHERD

I KNOW AT TIMES

I know at times we go thru things, but you know I'm going to always stay down, Because the only time I find myself happy, is when I'm talking to you, are when you're somewhere close around, And I hope you feel the same, because if you don't, everything that I'm saying might sound like a game, are kind of lame, But I don't have time for playing, I may be young, But I'm a whole man, And I know some, much older, that aren't able to do the things that I can, And I want you to understand, That I know that you are real to, That's why when it comes to you, there is nothing I won't do, I think we're a perfect team, And I plan to show you some things, in this life that you have never seen, Help you pursue your dreams, I owe you that much, because you showed me what real love means, And I know at times, I handle certain situations badly, But I gladly, except this position, as being your baby daddy!

I Believe In Love

    I believe in love, it's the strongest emotion ever heard of, so I would travel the seven seas, for the perfect love that's meant for me, that's meant to be, for all eternity. I believe in love, I haven't seen it, but I know exists. And I want to feel that feeling, that makes you feel like this, the butterflies and the happy cries, and you can tell when someone is in love there is a certain sparkle in their eyes, and a glow on their face, you can somehow see that they are in their happy place. A place of peace, so serene, and if you ever been in love, you know exactly what I mean. But to me it's still a dream, but I'm ready to awake. To find the love I need to find, and take the chance I need to take, it's never too late, so I'm counting on faith, to guide me on my way, and I'm yearning for the day, when I can truly say, I love you, and mean it, from the deepest part of my soul, where I can just let go, and let love take control. I just want Y'all to know, that I believe in love, I believe it's everything I need. Yes I believe, love is true happiness indeed, the perfect place to be. So I believe my true love is somewhere waiting just for me!

MY GIRL

It took some time for me to see, that your the only one for me, So many places I could be, But in your arms is where I'm free, You came and sparked a fire, that gave me the desire, To want to reach higher, and higher, That's My Girl, Your love is real not counterfeit, you will be right there, and I can count on it, With your since of humor and charm, and love, how you love me, and keep me warm, You're one of a kind, and I'm so glad that your mine, Yeah that's my girl, your beauty completes you, and I promise I need you, you need to, always be there, these are just A few words, to try to express how much I care, maybe one day you'll be my wife, because you bring life, to my world, that's why I thank God that, that's my girl!

A LETTER OF LOVE

I'm sending you a letter of love, because you set my heart on fire, You have me touching the sky, and I can't reach no higher, an intended desire, You are the perfect peddle of a delicate flower, And your love is a drug, that provides me with power, a radiant shower of passionate rain, A pleasure I feel, I just can't explain, It's like the dawn of the morning sun, shining thru a window pain, You're all that and a bag of chips, my cream filling, my honey dip, my chocolate vanilla shake, let me take me a sip, I'm losing my grip, and falling for you, could this be love I'm falling into, That's why I'm sending you this letter of love, because I think I'm addicted to your kisses and hugs, because you give me a buzz, I wish I knew what it was, that makes me feel like it does, You are magically delicious, and I wish this, moment could last for a life time, It's like I'm lost in a dream, and I don't want to awake until I know what it means, One thing I seen was my nose wide open, and I was just hoping, that you would touch me, that's why, this must be, The reason I'm writing this letter, this letter of love, To let you know that you are all I've been thinking of, Because you make me snap crackle pop, and you make my cinnamon toast, crunch, And I just love how you laugh, when I ask, can I have you for lunch, my sun kiss Hawaiian punch, what you ma call it, that kit cat a Nestlé crunch, Your brown sugar always makes it taste better, That's why I'm writing you this love letter!

SPECIAL FRIENDS

What I wouldn't do to see your face again, oh, how I would light up just to see you walking in, I had like the biggest crush on you back then, I was looking for love, but you just wanted to be friends, but I didn't mind playing that role, because if it were possible, I would have giving you my soul, my life in whole, but life is cold, knowing that I can't see you anymore, because we are worlds apart, and miles away, but in my prayers I pray, that I might see you again someday, I don't care if we're on a beach in the sand, or on a cloud in the skies, I just want to be there with you, staring at the glare in your eyes, I guess I never realized, just how much I really cared, and you don't know how much you love someone, until their no longer there, but if you love something, you have to set it free, just let it fly in the wind, and if what you had was genuine, it will find it's way back again, I never thought you dying, would hurt for so long, but it's going on fourteen years since you've been gone, but dear, I can feel you're here, that's the reason I wrote this poem, but I new your love was mine, and you would find your way home, even though, I won't ever see your beautiful face again, your memory will always live on thru my poems, as my special friend!

TRUE BEAUTY

See beauty is passing, but true beauty has passion, and it's everlasting, But looks are deceiving, they make the odds and ends uneven, you fall in love with beauty, but what is the real reason, What if the beauty doesn't last? Then you end up leaving, Beauty is like a season, it springs, then it falls, But tell me who can resist beauty, when beauty has called, But true love, is the most magnificent thing of all, the most beautiful thing I have ever saw, Because love, gives life to the heart, A genuine work of art, a masterpiece, that plays a major part, But beauty is passing, But true beauty has passion, and it's everlasting, True beauty comes from within, it doesn't bind or bend, But when it comes to the lust in us, the line is thin, But we find true beauty, when we find a real friend, That kind of beauty doesn't end, it last forever and ever, and just gets better and better, A life time of pleasure, a joy you can't measure, A priceless treasure, And a gift from God, So if you ever find true beauty in love, You better be grateful for it, Because beauty is passing, but true beauty has passion, and it's everlasting! "True Beauty"

"YOU'RE THE LOVE OF MY LIFE"

You're precious to me, like diamonds, gems and rubies, truly you're a beauty, you're my baby, my booby, when you met me you knew me, thoroughly and truly, you knew how to move me and groove me, how to upset and sooth me. And I'm glad that you choose me, and I choose you, cause without you, I couldn't imagine what I would do! That's why I thank God that I got you, because sometimes, it seems like, it's almost impossible to breathe with out you! You're a breath of fresh air, and I'm at my best, when you're there, you are the wind beneath my wing, you mean the world to me, you are my everything." YOU'RE THE LOVE OF MY LIFE"! That's why I need you to be, the first thing I see, when I wake up in the morning, and the last thing I see, before I go to sleep at night, And I love, how you love me right, you're a delicate delight, and you're perfect in my sight, that's why sometimes I just might, shake my head in "Ahu", because I'm still wondering, what all this love is for, you keep on loving me, tell I can't take no more, you're the one that I adore, my mi amour, the apple of my eyes, my ribbon in the skies, and I finally realized, that you're a heaven sent prize, so I must make you my wife! Will you marry me my love? THE LOVE OF MY LIFE!

LOVE

Love could be a beautiful thing, if you let it, if you respect it, protect it, and never forget it, set it high above, the price of rubies and gold, because love is something, you should hold close to your soul, something you should keep, that should never be sold, A treasure untold, we should plant seeds of love, and watch that love grow, but like other seeds, it's A time to reap and a time to sow, But I try to show love, thru the rain sleet and snow, because love can be A beautiful thing if it's real, A protective shield, A helping hand, that can help you heal, and make you feel, like the world is yours, like you got the green light, to paradise, and you're standing in front of the golden doors, and you are the VICTOR, because love has gave you victory, and love has possessed this power, throughout all history, don't just take it from me, take a look at love, and soon you'll see, that love, is the beauty of a flower, the smile of a friend, when you're in last place, then you come back and win, love is the tears you shed from loosing a friend, and turning from sin, because if you change your ways for God, you really got love then, because God gave us the sun, the moon, and the stars, and the emotions you feel, who ever you are, and the love you have, who ever it's for, love can be a beautiful thing, if you let it, if you respect it, protect it, and never forget it!

BEAUTY IS HER NAME

    Excuse me for a second, I think I recognize you from heaven, Or maybe we might have glanced at each other, from amongst the stars, so I wanted to meet you, so next time I see you, I would know who you are, she said " Beauty is my name" she's a picture of perfection I just can't explain, like a mixture of pleasure and pain, or trying to measure the rain, I still remember the first time I saw this beautiful Goddess, I tried my hardest, to avoid this, feeling I felt, cause she has a smile, long as the Nile, that can make a man melt, and as long as I've been living, I haven't seen such a glorious vision, she gives off a radiant light, like when the sun has risen, I was so intrigued, she left me with the feeling, that she had everything that I need, indeed, she is a beauty to my eyes, Beauty is her name, my love above the skies, the color of her eyes, compliment the earth, and God hasn't made a thing yet, that can add up to her worth, she is pure perfection, her presence, is an expression, of her affection, such essence and charm, like a cool wind when it's warm, she'll send chills up your spine, and leave goose bumps on your arm, Beauty is her name, and heaven is her home, she also has this shadow of darkness, that can start this, swirl from a world wind, and make your world spin, I that's the reason she has trouble dealing with most men, they just can't understand her, because sometimes she goes through some things there not strong enough to handle, from heaven is where she came, some call her mother nature, but Beauty is her name!

WHOLE HEARTEDLY

I loved you whole heartedly, like you were apart of me, cause I thought, when two people became one, that's how it aught to be, now it's hard to see, how you can just act so differently. Like they say "All good things come to an end", but as close as we were, I thought we would at least remain friend's, but naw, you chose to cut off all ties, and left me to deal with all the hurt and the lies, you waged war on me, like I was your enemy, someone you despised, but I really wasn't that surprised, I'm just looking at everything as a whole, trying to rationalize. I'm so tired of asking questions, I already know the answer to, I closed my eyes, to a lot of things that you were doing, that you didn't know I knew. And in a lot of ways, I'm glad we're thru, cause plenty of times, you were out of control, And I didn't know what to do. And I can't lie and say that I don't miss you, because that's not true, one of my biggest reason I had for living, was loving you. And I know as time passes, all wounds will heal, but as of now, nothing can change the pain that I feel, cause I loved you whole heartedly, like you were apart of me, because I thought when two people became one that's how it aught to be!

POET TREE IN MOTION   ROYAL SHEPHERD

CLOSER

Let me come closer, and maybe then we'll have closure, and I might just get to know you, and show you, just what kind of man I could be, or you might be the one, that can make a man out of me, slowly, we will take it one day at a time, I will get to know about your life, and you will get to know about mines, as we become closer, I will find out, about what you like, and what you don't, what you will, and what you won't except, and we'll grow, deeper and deeper in debt, and I will give you more and more of me, tell we have no secrets left, one step, closer, we will let the moments of life be our chauffeur, and I'll try and do everything I told you, I'll give you my heart, but I will need your shoulder, to guide me through life, when I'm not sober, a true helping hand, when this young man gets older, and for you, I'll be your soldier, I'm under your command, you make the blueprints, and I'll fulfill the plans, I will do everything that I can, so we can begin, to come closer, in sync, what you think, I think, when you move, I move, like an instinct, on the brink, of becoming one, we will keep on building, tell all the buildings done, And we still , will always remember when all the feelings begun! AS WE BECOME CLOSER!

I DID IT FOR YOU

I did it for you, da da, dada da, I did it for you, yea, ay ay, a, First off God, I did it for you, because I love how you made me, I was just a thug, selling drugs, and you came and save me, you made me, "marvelous", "magnificent", "manufeic", you made me meek, with a mean streak, you gave me a smile, that can light up a room, always well mannered, always well groomed, always in tuned on life, knowing the difference, between, wrongs, and rights, not perfect, but precise, genuine just right, That's why I did it for you, da da dada, da, that's why I did it for you, yea, ay ay, a, I did it for you Mom's, because you always believed, you gave me everything that I need, the gift to succeed, you showed me how to follow, so I would be strong enough to lead, so you are my Queen indeed, That's why I did it for you, da da, dada, da, that's why I did it for you, yea, aa, a, I did it for you son, because you're the light of my life, and I couldn't go on, letting you see me do wrong, so daddy had to do something right, and I'm not saying, that I'm winning the game, but I'm fighting the good fight, that's why I'm here tonight, standing in front of this crowd, daddy had to do something, so I could make my baby proud, That's why I did it for you, da da, dada da, that's why I did it for you, yea, aa, a, And to everyone that I greet with a firm handshake and a hug, the one's who knew what it was, when I was out there, selling drugs, the one's that never judged, or held a grudge, but instead showed me love, I did it for you, now it's time to do it for me, to see how far I can fly, and how free I can be, That's why I did it for you, da da, dada, da, that's why I did it for you, yea, aa, ay !

KISS ON THE CHEEK

What's small but it's special, soft but it's sweet, it's very familiar, but it's some what unique, You know silly, It's a kiss on the cheek, That's the way the French greet, mercy, we we, then their lips, and cheeks meet, oh, what a treat, the kiss on the cheek, it's used for all type of greetings, family reunions, dates, the smile on a babies face, and the first time meeting, sneaking and cheating, around the school yard, thought you were being slick, but everybody at school saw it, I remember being young, I had the biggest crush, when she kiss me on the cheek, oh how she made me blush, and she said friends was God's special plan for us, that was years ago months and even weeks, but I will never forget that first kiss on the cheek, what about the ultimate kiss on the cheek good bye, where you can taste the love, from the tears that they cry, my my my, some people are so shy, that's the ones, you have to give a kiss on the cheek, on the sly, a husband and wife, after she has adjusted his tie, It's also, the kiss you give to encourage your kids to try, that's something, that no one can deny, so if you haven't done this in awhile, give someone a big old kiss on the cheek, just to see them smile !

LOVE IS A CRAZY GAME

Love is a crazy feeling, and a dangerous game to play, But if you ever find a real love, that love will save the day, So try your best, not to just let that kind of love slip away, Cause sometimes love can grow and mature, Then put you in a place where you are safe and secure, And almost sure, That you will live life happily ever after, and never have to, search your heart for love again, But then, what if you don't find that special one you've been waiting for, And the one that you have, has you searching for more, Just beat down to the floor, and you just don't know, If their faking, or if their real, about the feelings that they feel, Now you're wondering will you're heart, ever be able to heal, if you don't make it through this crazy ordeal, And all you can do is pray, Because love is a crazy feeling, and a dangerous game to play, But if you keep your heart pure, I'm almost sure, you'll find that perfect love someday!

PRESENCE FROM THE WINDOW

I can still feel your presence from the window, when the wind blow, when I come to think about it, you were so sentimental, but you were very outgoing though, and trust worthy, I guess that's why I loved you so, you always let your yeses mean yes, and your no's mean no. You told me that love was real, then you showed me how love can feel, even though you're gone my love is strong still, it's your smile, I miss the most, and then it's your eyes, that's the port hole, to the soul, and you know the soul, never lies. But sometimes my soul cries, from missing you so much, your sweet kisses and soft touch. Can't nobody take your place, oh how I miss your beautiful face, so much glory, such grace, without you in my life, my heart is just taking up space. But I can still feel your presence, from the window, when the wind blow. And that's got me asking God, why did you have to go? And what am I still here for? For the life of me, I just don't know, but I'm almost sure, you had to go, to prepare a way for the lost, and you were always so giving, I know you some how tried to pay the cost, I can almost picture you, trying to put a good word into the boss, gently asking, can you lay his sins down on the cross, you are my, picture of perfection, of love and affection, all you wanted in return, was love and protection, I guess I ended up failing, in that section, maybe that's why I can still feel your presence, from the window, when the wind blow, cause I'm not sure, that I'm doing the things, that God sent me here for. But I want you to know, that your presence, is a present, nice and pleasant, and just in case, I don't make it in, because of sin, you have been my heaven. That's why I can still feel your presence, from the window, when the wind blow!

CHAPTER THREE

LET MY PEOPLE GO

Martin Luther King had a dream, but me I have a vision, of me talking to the Pharaoh, telling him, let my people go free from prison, and I hope that he listens, or who else will save us, from this modern day plantation, called incarceration. All the revolutionaries are dead, all we have left are the words that they said, they spoke of things like hope, freedom, and equality, but Ain't no hope of being free and equal in this world for me, especially a black male with an x, or a father on child support, their taking half of our checks, what will they do next, it seems like, the government and women, have waged war against males, making all kinds of laws, just to keep us in jail. What are they thinking, their locking up brothers with Doctrine degrees, for driving and drinking, now this is the part that really sounds funny, it's a crime, because I help make a child, but I don't have any money, then they send me to jail, and take the rest of my family from me. What I'm saying, is that I've been praying, that all men come together, cause in this day an age that's the only way things are going to get better. God made males, to be the head and not the tail, to be fruitful and excel, and to stay for away from jail. Martin Luther King had a dream but me I have a vision, and I'm telling the Pharaoh, to let my people go free from prison, what's going on with these women, making all these false calls to the laws, putting these guys life on pause, then they send mail, and visit the jail everyday, that has to be one of the most evil games, I have ever seen played, right is right and wrong is wrong, if you are not getting along, pack your things and move on, don't send that man to jail, because the love is gone, Martin had a dream, but me

I have a vision, of me asking these women, to please stop sending these brothers to prison, And I can see where you women are loosing to, Because their sending us to jail. but their using you! LET MY PEOPLE GO!

I DON'T BELIEVE

I don't believe you cheated on me, sneaking around behind my back, and you claim that you're real, but tell me, how real is that, and you say that you love me, but where is all the love at, I know I can forgive you but I know I won't forget, this relationship should be over but I'm not ready to give up yet, above everything, you were one of the best women I ever met, but my heart is sore, and I'm not sure I can trust you after that, I guess it's because you didn't have no kind of respect, you had the audacity, to walk pass me, with that big old passion mark on your neck, what was I supposed to do next, give you a big old hug and kiss. Never in my wildest dreams, would I have ever thought, that you would do me like this, it hurts just to picture you, in the arms of another man, it's hard but I can, that's what makes it, so hard to understand, I play that scene in my mind, over, and over again, and what hurts me the most, was to find out, that it was one of my friends. How could the both of Y'all, just sit in my face and pretend, when will all the madness ever end. I still can't believe, I was that naive, back then! I don't believe. You were my family, and a friend, so how would I have not let you in, down on your luck, with no place to go, I can still picture the look on your face, the day you came knocked at my door. You were looking lost and frantic, I welcome you in with open arms and told you try not to panic, but somehow you took that for granite, and violated my trust, pursuing your lust, you put a lot of bad blood between us, Family, I had love for you, for real, now when I think about you, love is the last emotion that I feel, I DON'T BELIEVE

I'M RUNNING OUT OF TIME!

I've seen hours, turn into days, and days turn into weeks, and weeks turn into months and months turn into years, I've seen faith turn into fears, and smiles turn into tears, after everything I've seen, I'm trying to see what I have here, I know I have God, and my life, my body and soul, the love of my family and friends, and sometimes, my friends I'm not sure, but what I do know. You get what you give, and you reap, what you sow. And everything happens for a reason, a season or a life time, and everybody, everything, Ain't happening like mine, but we all, are in a race, and we're running out of time. That's why I'm trying to keep a steady pace, and stay in my lane, because in these days, people play some dangerous games, I know you like the sunshine, but be ready for the rain, and we all want to be loved, but with love comes pain. It's a time for everything, a time to live, and a time to die, a time to laugh and a time to cry, all in all, we just all trying to get by. While we pay our dues, but we can't waste no time, because we have no time to lose, cause I seen hours, turn into days, and days turn into weeks, and weeks turn into months, and months turn into years, then all those moments started looking like the end was near. So I decided to slow down. Because I was winning the race, BUT I WAS RUNNING OUT OF TIME!

AM I MY BROTHER'S KEEPER

Am I my brothers keeper, I am if he kept me, if I was blind, and he help me see, or if I was locked up and he set me free, then I guess I would be, my brothers keeper, but then it gets deeper, how long shall I be his crutch, and should I still be my brothers keeper if he only help me this or that much, but my other brothers help me more, he was only the wind beneath my wing, the others help me sore, but his heart was always pure, genuine, but that was years ago, way back when, plus I have moved on now, and I've made new friend's, and should I still help my brother, if his help involves my ends, well I guess that depends, are what if he needed a place to lay his head, and he said, "he'll take the floor, he doesn't even need a bed", would you let your brother in, or would you give him some pocket change, instead, mind you, this is your brother that really broke bread, his cash, cars and clothes he always would share it, what if, he really didn't even need a place to go, He was just dying inside, and didn't nobody know, wow! Now I know for show that I haven't been, but the next time my brother comes knocking, I'm going to let him in, because the last time he came, I gave him some pocket change, and he ended up going to the pin, but the next time, I will console him, and give him some direction, and if my brother needs a hug, I will give him that affection, because I remember when I was crying and dying inside, he would stop everything he was doing, and come right on by, and that little talk, and that little time, always seem to ease my mind, no I haven't been my brother's keeper, but I think it's time to start trying! I AM MY BROTHER'S KEEPER

SERIOUSLY FOR REAL

I just love to see two women, rubbing touching and feeling, but what I don't understand, Y'all are trying to stand hand and hand, and there's always a man willing, sitting at the house with his hands in his pants chilling, and if your man piece game isn't strong, take dude to the freak store and strap him one on, because he is going to start getting suspicious, if every time he gets home, you and your bestie are always gone, He gone be like "what the hell is going on", "Seriously For Real", But this is what I can't stand, to see two boys playing, man, man, man, I'm just saying, Ain't no dude can do what a women can, First of all Y'all just faking it, I don't care if you're giving it or taking it, Boy you know that's nasty, when they walk by I can almost smell the poo past me, Please forgive me for speaking rashly, but if you trying to hit some ass, get it from Ashley or Dianne, because it's just to many women out here to be messing with a man, That's the part I don't understand, "Seriously For Real", You dudes dressing in drag, and your breath smelling like a dragon, my girls got there pants sagging, bulldagging, all on face book bragging, stop all the acting, Because you put off as needy, and you just give yourself up so easy, And if you are sleeping with a woman and a man, you are just straight up greedy, And I Don't Mean To Offend Anyone, I'm Just Expressing How I Feel, But I Am Serious, For Real!

WHAT ARE WE DOING HERE?

What are we doing here, How did we get lost, I guess we just kept making bad choices and wrong turns, so our signals got crossed, We kept holding on, but we kept on falling off, Our heads were kind of hard, which left our ass kind of soft, We have a lot of learning to do, and a lot of lonely valleys that we must travel through, But we were moving kind of fast, not knowing where the road ahead would take us, We were just a couple of rollers and shakers, Trying to get away from the haters and fakers, But I guess it's safe to say, We just didn't have enough money to move, and we didn't have enough money to stay, So we were on a road to nowhere, moving at a fast pace, And was so caught up in the thrill of the chase, we couldn't even see that it all was a waste, Trying to save ass, we had to lose face, And that left everything a little out of place, Now we are wondering WHAT ARE WE DOING HERE, where did we go wrong, we didn't like it where we were, but this is not where we belong, Stuck at a dead end, and our gas is all gone, WHAT ARE WE DOING HERE, WHERE DID WE GO WRONG, but I guess this is what you go thru, trying to make it on your own!

HOW COULD I?

Are you okay , I worried about you all last night, And I know that it's not right, Being concerned about another man's wife, But I really believe that you're worth the fight, mi vela loco, my crazy life, I know, I just can't pretend, Because in these days that we're living in, You're either mice or men, And I know it's A sin to covet another man's wife, But you're a delicate flower, that hasn't been treated properly, And I want to see you grow, And I'm going to let you know, That you're beautiful, And you deserve so much more, Maybe I'm just talking out the side of my head, To me you are a Queen, and one of the most amazing women I have ever seen, To wake up to you every morning would be like a dream, Aren't you tired of all that fussing and fighting, Getting knocked over the head, wouldn't you like some kissing and hugging, real loving instead, To see you crying and hurting, is breaking my heart, tearing me apart, And I know that you have to leave, but I wish it were possible for you to stay, How could I have ever, falling in love with another man's wife this way, Before she left all I could do was hold her, While the pain from her tear drop stains dampen my shoulder, I didn't see her again tell we were much older, And she informed me that her marriage was over, But her heart was hard and she was scarred, She disguised her pain like a soldier from war, I'm not sure, but I think it hurt me more, to see her this way, I keep her in my prayers, But we never seen each other again after that day!

DEAF AND BLIND

Believe none of what you hear, and only some of what you see, because usually, a wrong perception can mislead you and me, That's why we have to be, on our P's and Q's, Because folks can deceive you, by feeding you false news, And they be so amused, by giving you false information that you're unable to use, That's why you have to stay away from those kind, The kind that makes fun and lie, and tries to leave you in the blind, pay them no mind, no mind at all, Because they are the ones dropping stumbling blocks to make you fall, They are wolves in sheep's clothing, searching for prey, So be mindful of their tricks and slick games they try to play, They say that there is a trick born everyday, And this might be true, But you don't have to listen to these tricks, and let the joke be on you, So use your common sense, and confidence, as a weapon, And when you see those clowns, coming around, you get to stepping, Don't even give them the opportunity to plant negative seeds, The envy the greed, don't be deceived, you have everything that you need, A strong spirit and a sound mind, the rest of your gifts you'll find in time, So don't believe none of what you hear, and only some of what you see, That's the blueprints to peace, and the place you need to be!

YOU NEVER KNOW

At one point I was homeless, living out on the street, broke as a joke, not knowing where I would get my next meal to eat, I know you are like that could never be me, But in actuality, you don't know what trials you might meet, are what things you might do, Are what God is going to take you through, If only you knew, But we don't, we don't even know what we might say, are what can lead us to lose our way, It's somewhere between, a broken heart, and a dark dream, That can almost make you lose everything, And your friends will be like, He use to be one of the ones, a son of a gun, what is he on, and what has he done, But me, I was just moving to fast, having too much fun, Making a lot of money, but then I ended up with none, Hanging out under bridges, picking cans out of ditches, I just couldn't catch a grip, on the ball that life pitches, What I really needed, was someone to talk to, a few minutes of there time, Because I was just so confused, about to lose my mind, I needed some direction, some love and affection, But I wrote this for your protection, and awareness, So you don't lose focus, and start being careless, This is my message to you, You never know what you might do, are what God might take you through, A few hard times or two, The new person under the bridge, Just might be you, YOU NEVER KNOW!

DON'T PLAY THE PART OF A LOSER!

How can I win playing the part of a loser, and that's not what I'm use too, I probably couldn't even fool you, I have to play the part of a teacher or a ruler, or maybe something even cooler, like a genius or a jeweler, somebody with the tools to, make something happen, a corporal or a captain, someone with power, to hire and fire, clean out your desk, you have about an hour, I have to be the best that makes moves, because people with less has so much to prove, and nothing to lose, always saying their just paying their dues, then you see them on the news, looking confused, lost with no clues, playing the role of a fool, is just straight up cruel, please choose someone else for that role, don't make me the mule, how can you win playing the part of a loser, a user, someone that use to   something, now it's gone, and they are thinking all wrong, singing that same old song, if I would have did this, or if I would have did that, in fact, you wouldn't of did jack, if I wore suits and slacks, would that make me a Mack, that's not a bad part, I wouldn't mind playing that, But I know life is not a movie at all, and sometimes we go thru things, that makes it hard to stand tall, I'm here to tell Y'all, not to lose heart, since life is not a movie, you get to choose your parts, so be smart, when you choose, and know that you can't win, Playing a part where you lose!

DANGEROUS MINDS

  I have seen some of the most angriest kinds, lock down and confined, for doing all sorts of crimes, some do the time, some just sit around and wine, always crying, cause there sick and tired of trying, but this is only one type of dangerous mind, some don't show the signs, they keep you in the blind, until they put you in a bind, and it's a thin line between crazy and sane, some they love pleasure, but their pleasure is pain, others are kind of plain, they talk to themselves like their playing a little game, now these are the minds I can't explain, what the situation is, they are always filled with tears, their mind tells them things that keep them with fears, and they want to kill themselves, because they think the end is near, they hear voices that tell them to take off their clothes, what's going on in their mind only God knows, then some just have a killer instinct, and they think, that they need to kill just to feel right, and they can't sleep at night, unless they have taking a persons life, others are simply out of control, running around loose, drug induced, about to loose their soul, some of these folks are sick, I mean straight up file, grown perverted people, that want to have sex with a child, one of the most dangerous mind's I have ever saw, the ones practicing homosexuality, an abomination under God's great law, my people don't let Satan confuse you, to use you as apart of his sick little games, So if you find yourself doing any of these things, you need to check yourself, and really try to change, because you're all the way out of line, These are signs, of a dangerous mind!

HAND OUTS

     My mother raised me to be a man, to buy what I need if I can don't waste time, staying in line trying to get a help hand. But now I really understand, cause I see everybody got there hand out for the life of me I can't see what that's all about. cause what they eat don't make me burp so I don't mind getting off my behind to go work. But some people think imma jerk, cause I won't give all mines away. But I got bill to pay and they to busy trying to play. That's why I learned to separate myself from people that's to concern with other people wealth. How can me and you have the same job make the same pay but you always need some help you don't see nothing wrong with that picture. But you always coming to me, wanting something for free. You must think I fix ya. But I'm not fixing to give you nothing but some advice. You need to start saving your change, and do some better things, with your life. Don't take this wrong, in my life I've made plenty mistakes. But imma try to come up on my own cause I know what lil time it takes and I have, accepted a helping hand from a friend a time or two. They no I don't play no games, when it comes to change, and I'll do the same for you. If you always need and never help, maybe you need, to check yourself. You know what I'm talking bout don't be caught on the spot being the man with his hands out.

SAVE YOURSELF

I finally found the way to be free, give God praise, change my ways, and stop letting people save me, because actually they can't save you at all, most of the time, they are just there to pick you up when you fall, but when you learn how to save yourself, this can save your life, first you have to put your trust in the Lord, Jesus Christ, and then believe, that he laid down your sins on the cross as he was sacrificed, for those who believe, he has prepared a place for us in paradise, That's why I except Jesus as my personal Lord and savior, and a constant help, so when I pray, he leads the way, so I can save myself, he gave us the our father's prayer, so we can know that our father's there, in our time of need, See Jesus thought us how to follow so we would be wise enough to lead, plant seeds and recruit, to go out and bare fruit, inspire a whole group, to instill the desire for truth, in our youth, thru Jesus Christ we have proof, That God is real, so we should know by his stripes that we are healed, now it's time to build, and let the truth be revealed, if you see someone hungry, try to help them with a meal, I've been full, and I've been hungry so I know how they both feel, I know it's good to do good, but you must save yourselves still!

OPINIONS

Some people need to learn how to keep their opinions to their self, cause if a situation is already bad, Your bad opinions won't help, when you need to be getting, your own house in order, cleaning the dust off your shelf, By taking care of your family and your health, and stop worrying about everybody else, Cause on the real, you still got to deal, with the hand you were dealt, But if you only knew how you sound, when you act a fool, ridicule, and talk down, Cause you fell into a rut, and got ship wreck and stuck out of luck, Now you want to pass the buck, By making others look bad, Cause you broke and mad, tried to come up too fast and fell flat on your ass, Now you thinking everybody going to laugh, So you put on a facade, and a mask, But tell me how long do you think this little charade, is going to last, And that's sad, mane, cause you had the audacity to actually make other people apart of your pain, By trying to blemish there image, and slander there names, What kind of sick little games or you playing ,What you need to do is learn how to start praying, Instead of always staying, in somebody else's mess, You must think breaking someone down will somehow help you progress, But I guess, if you just, can't use your words to help, then you need to keep your opinion's to yourself!

POET TREE IN MOTION   ROYAL SHEPHERD

ANGER

Anger is a deadly disease, That is contracted by selfishness, jealousy and insecurities, if you poses, any of these, you may be in danger, of this evil disease, That we call anger, Here are some of the symptoms to be aware of, verbal and mental, abuse, and lack of love, emotions change from the way they was, inflicting pain and hurt on others, This is what anger does, being brood, with an attitude just because, It's a passionate displeasure for people and things, This is the evil that anger will bring, hatefulness that causes dismay, only low self esteem and failed dreams can leave you this way, And the only way to be healed is to kneel and pray, put away the past and stand fast for a better day, Then God will send you love, which is gentle and kind, and the power that love has will put the past behind, Love is a precious flower and a passionate song, That fills you with joy tell the anger is gone!

CHAPTER FOUR

ONE BAD NIGHT

    I can't imagine, how horrible it is to have your innocents stolen, but you don't have to continue in the direction that the dice has been rolling, it's your life, that this painful night is controlling, you're letting the lost of your purity, leave you with low self esteem an insecurity, but don't let your past be the author of your future, you need to search thru your life, so you can see what might suit you, put away the trash that you're use to, that makes you feel like a looser, and take of that mask, it's only a reflection of your past, that's what has you moving so fast, and promiscuous, the old you, was nothing like this, you held on to that pain for long enough, the stress the strain and all that other stuff, now it's finally time to let it all go, you've been thru hell and that's for sure, but even if you stump a seed in the ground it's bound to grow, nobody has the right, to do what this person did to you that night, but you can't let that horrible act, hold you back, for the rest of your life, first start off by burying that part of you that died, and bring to life the beauty that you have inside, put away your pride, and open up your eyes, so you can see that the sky is the limit, but in order to win the game, you have to be in it, so don't be timid, because God gave you life, with his power, so as long as you are living and breathing, you're God's precious flower, so stay away from dark hearted people, with evil intent, and hateful ways, because they were only made, for the judgement days, and if you always let God, be your shining light, you won't have to ever worry about another bad night!

MEN OF HONOR

We need to be men of honor, prestige, God has already equipped us with everything we need, the gift to succeed. It's not a time to follow, it's a time to lead, plant seeds, and what you can't get done in will, get done in deed. Please take heed, and be a man of honor, Strong stable, willing and able, to take care of anything that arises, especially surprises, See God made us in his image, so we are the wises, now apply this, to your everyday mission, stand firm and in position, use your intuition, and your ambition, that creates a tough Christian! A man of honor, a scholar, that knows the meaning of a dollar, a friend, that knows how to lend a helping hand, a mighty man, quick to start praying! what I'm saying, is! We need to be genuine, real, set apart, a master piece, a piece of work, a work of art! Having some sort of God, in your heart, with these qualities, you can't come up short, being a man of honor , a man of power, Stand tall and tower, teach and try to reach, strengthen the weak, before the final hour, be a blessing in disguise, that comes from the blessing in the skies, don't let life pass you by, trying to be like those other guys, reach for the skies, reach for the prize, show the youth where their salvation lies, a man of honor I better be, from all my Mom's instilled in me, morals and integrity! So what you see in me, is a man of honor!

HOLD ON

You have to hold on, after you have took all that you can take, keep your hopes up high and alive until you establish faith. It's never too late to make all things new, you just have to get yourself together and figure out what you really need to do, trust me this is true, if you hold on and keep going, God will see you thru. Be steadfast not easily moved, and leave yourself some room, some room to improve, cause change is a challenge that you have to be up for, in order to move up more, into your season, and always remember that everything happens for a reason. But first you must start believing, in something higher than yourself, when times get hard, call on the Lord, because he's a constant help. When everything is going wrong, and all my friends are gone, I call on the Lord, and he helps me hold on. He's my leader, my over seer, he's the healer of my life, because Christ paid the price, by being the living sacrifice, that's why I give him praise everyday and every night, because when I was wrong he made me right, when I was in the dark, he gave me light, and when I was weak he made me strong, so I could hold on, and win the fight

I JUST WANT TO BE

I just want to be, so strong, that nothing can disturb my peace, I want to be healthy and happy, and make my finances increase, I just want to be the one, that makes folks feel, that there's nothing they can't do, Somehow show them the sunny side of things, that can make their dreams come true, I want to be the one, to inspire them to think only of the best, to work only for the best, and to expect nothing less than the best, and to be, just as enthusiastic, about someone else's success, I just want to be the one, who can move on from my past mistakes, and do what it takes, to make the moves I need to make, so one day, I will be able to be great, I want to be the one, that greets everyone I meet, with a smile, stop an encourage a child, every once in a while, Basically, I just want to be, too large for worry, too noble for anger, too strong for fear, and too blessed, to be stressed, and let trouble come near, I guess I'm just a want to be!

DON'T DROP THE BALL

At one point of my life, people thought I had dropped the ball for sure, but I was just dribbling it, to reach closer to my goal, take it from me I played enough games to know, if you love something, you have to let it go, but if it comes back to you it's really yours for sure, I learned I could do things better if I just took things slow, clean up the game that I have, and try to learn a little more, So I started looking at the bigger picture, so I could see what I was sent here for, and as I start looking at the course of my life, I started seeing things clearer, my wrongs and my rights, And what I found, is that you can't get distracted by the shining lights, the debts or the heights, because they were only put there, so you could set your sights, on something better, to set you on high, so you won't have to settle, so after you have persevered, you could obtain the metal, But whatever you do, don't drop the ball, Be ready to get back in the game, before the ref has called, his final call, after all is all, know you have done the best that you can, and you can still stand tall, equipped for whatever comes your way, just in case you lose the battle, be prepared to win the war the next day, and if the coach puts you in the game be ready to play, ready to give it everything you got, And know that if you're in control of the ball in the final seconds, that you will hit the winning shot, JUST DON'T DROP THE BALL!

POET TREE IN MOTION   ROYAL SHEPHERD

THE MORE YOU GROW

The more you grow, the more fake friends you attract, I've been there, and done that, and I'm not going back, See when you start getting money, people don't know how to act, In fact, they start running around trying to find where you're at , I can't fall off track like that, so I stay on the run, If you're not my day one, then our fake friendship is done, now you're just a fan, on the outside looking in, They be like "Hey boy where you been", I've been hiding from your tail, because when I was going thru hell, "you were hiding then" And you don't have to be, an Emmie nominee or nothing like that, Folks will start hunting you down, simply because you received your income tax, I'm just speaking facts, The more you grow, the more fake friends you attract, But I have been there, and done that, and I'm not going back, But I'm learning how to feed folks with a long handle spoon, Because God has built me a house, but in this house it's not that many rooms, There is no room for lies or deceit, or fake friends trying to cheat, Cause in reality, the same folks that smile in your face when you're on your feet, is the same folks that laugh at you, when you kicked out on the street, The reason I know, is because I've been there before, with no one to call, and nowhere to go, But as soon as I started to grow, Here come all the fake friends knocking at my door, That's why I don't care if folks think I'm acting funny, Because when I had no ends, I had no friends, So I made amends, with my money, That's why I stack, like I stack, and act like I act, Because I know, The more you grow, the more fake friends you attract, I've been there, and done that, and I'm not going back!

OPPORTUNITY

Opportunity awaits me, I'm going to enjoy the ride, to the places where opportunity is about to take me, I'm going to try not to stumble and keep myself humble, While I wait for my number to arise, and in time I'll get my prize, in do season, I'll find, my purpose my reason, For living, until then I'll just play the cards I've been giving, The hand that I was dealt, Yet in still trying to learn from my mistakes, of when I missed the big breaks, And know I had what it took, But I just didn't use the tools that it takes, Yes opportunity awaits, So I won't give up, I'll keep on trying, and do mine, by faith, One moment at a time, always observing what I'm doing, while pursuing a peace of mind, Trying to stay focus, in the direction of my goals, Being persistent and patient, tell everything unfolds, Like the peddle of a rose, in the proper setting, it somehow seems to glow, so full of life it may seem like it grows, Then all it needs is an opportunity and it will be chose, That's how I know, that opportunity awaits me, so I'm just going to enjoy the ride, And see how far opportunity will take me!

NEVER STOP TRYING

It's never a waste of time, trying to do better, in these days, we need to find ways to get ourselves together, even though we are sinners, what lye's before us, and behind us, are only small things, compared to what lye's within us, but if you look you'll find, a happy heart and a peace of mind, it only takes a lil time, so never stop trying, cause in the end you will find, that you are truly divine, a special design, made to stand out, one of a kind, but I still remember when I was least in line, I didn't have a pot to piss in or a window to throw it out of, nobody showed me no love, no kisses no hugs, no exaggeration that's exactly how it was, I couldn't get a ride to the store, a cigarette to blow, no one had no love to show, I guess that's why, I don't feel the same about people no more, I don't owe them a hello, and if I do tell them something, I tell them where they can go, and that's to hell if they don't pray, and it's not on me, if they decide to slide that way, that's why I have to stay focus, because it's easy to get confuse, and loose everything like hocus pocus, wasting your time playing games with these jokers, don't be blind and fall behind, keep on moving and never stop trying, so don't ever give up, hold on, even when things seem to be going wrong, stay strong, you can win the fight, before long, a fire will ignite, that will bring a change in your life, and you will see that everything will be alright. So never stop trying!

I HAVE SEEN THAT FACE BEFORE

I have seen your face before, the stress, pain and agony, it's the same face I see sometimes, when I look in the mirror at me, such a lonely place to be, so much anguish an grief, in need of pain relief, hoping the pain would cease, and you can somehow find peace, Yes, I've been there before, such an empty road, seems like your about to explode, because you have no place to unload, the pressure the pain, almost going insane, but steady trying to maintain, wondering if you will ever regain, your self control, your at a place in your life, where everything is so cold, and all the doors are close, your dying inside, and nobody knows, I have seen your face before, several times, for a while I was thinking that , that face was mine, at that time I fell to my knees and started crying, while I was praying, I was saying, please God send me a sign, that can help me find me, and please set me free, from depression, low self esteem and insecurities, and please guide my path, to keep me from being in places I don't need to be, God heard my prayers and he rescued me, now when I see that face of agony and pain, I start praying, that I don't have to ever where that face again!

POET TREE IN MOTION   ROYAL SHEPHERD

I'M GOING ALL THE WAY!

I made up my mind, that I won't let nothing hold me down this time, I'm going to steadfast and pray, And I'm not worried about nothing these folks have to say, are the little games, they like to play, I'm going all the way, I have my mind made up, and my eyes are focused on God, my spirit is on fire so I'm not falling for it, for the first time in my life I can see things all the way thru, it's no if ands or buts, I know exactly what to do, and that's to stay true to God, and stay true to myself, take care of my health, and help who I can help, watch my steps and stay humble, you know Satan, is hating, waiting to make me stumble, so I must step out on faith, and make no mistakes, and do what it takes, to get my project completed, Because I finally found out, God was all that I needed, So now I'm going all the way, there's no looking back, the kingdom is calling, and heaven is at hand, God made me a promise, that I had a mansion in the promise land, Lord knows, it's been hard out here trying to make it on my own, that's why I'm glad that my dad, up in heaven has prepared for me a home, thru my ends an my outs my ups and my downs, I held strong and maintained, now I'm on my way to gain my crown, I'M GOING ALL THE WAY!

EXPRESSION

A poet is a person of expression, a blessing, and if you listen long enough, you might just learn a lesson, but that's just my suggestion, cause some spoken word, can make you even question, your whole way of life, but it's only you who, who knows what you do, if it's wrong or right, but the words of a poet, just might enlighten, the things you have going on tonight, so I invite, you into the mind of a poet, our words are a token, and we are highly, out spoken, and we just love to leave the mic smoking, and leave some things soaking, in your heart, that can either, build you up, or tear you apart, Because a poet, is a person of expression, a blessing, and if you listen long enough, you just might learn a lesson, but that's just my suggestion, cause some spoken words, can make you even question, the life you've been living, or give you drive, are you might just realize, that you've been getting driven, that your marriage is a prison, you can't talk on the phone, when their there, your alone, you love to love, but your love is always gone, for someone this is hitting home, That's the kind of stuff, them poets be on, they can touch a tender spot in your soul, that can make you lose control, But poets are just people of expression, a blessing, but some times they want to learn some of your lessons, hear some of your confessions, so the poet in you, can meet the poet in me, and I will show you how to be free, by releasing yourself thru your poetry, Then you will be a person of expression, a blessing, and if you keep saying poetry long enough, you just might teach some lessons!

EVERYTHING IS GONNA BE ALRIGHT!

      If God says the same everything is going to be alright, with his will and his might, We were built just right, It's just like, following instruction to baking a cake, You whip it up, put it in, then pull it out that's all it takes, And the belief that everything will be alright, that's what we call faith, But you must take action in your beliefs, quit being just Indians, try to become a chief, Then your faith and strength will start to increase, Release all the anger that you have in your heart, That kind of energy can really tear you apart, So be smart, stay away from anything that will bring you down, If you see trouble coming your way, you have to move around, Submit yourself to God, resist the devil, and he shall flee, And your father who art in heaven shall set you free, "I'M JUST A NOBODY, TRYING TO TELL EVERYBODY, ABOUT SOMEBODY, WHO CAN SAVE ANYBODY, So know that everything will be alright, as long as you remain strong, God will be right by your side, to give you comfort, tell all the pain is gone, Even though the roads you've been traveling on have been kind of rough, But it has made you strong enough, to reach the top, with God on your side you just can't be stopped, So keep on climbing, don't let nothing hold you down, even though life can be such a lonely place sometimes, So hide yourself in the shelter of the most high, it's safety there and peace of mind, whatever you need, you seem to find, So just keep on trying, And everything will be alright, right on time!

CHAPTER FIVE

BACK IN THE OLD DAYS !

I remember back in the old days, jamming that Frankie Beverly and Maze, and the O jays, and we wore them old jay's, the ones that look like snakeskin, everybody was rocking those back then, that's back when, Coca-Cola and Mickey mouse sweaters were cool, and everybody had to have a beeper on at school, how about starter jackets and no back caps, I think Easy E and them niggers with attitudes, put that on the map, what about those shirts, with the Izod logo, guess jeans, and polo, but if you wore wranglers and pro wings, that was a no no, if that was the type of gear you wore, you rode solo, talking about rolling, what about roller skating at the skating ring, lil love letters, doing the dating thing, that's when rap music was off the chain, Scarface and Willi D, these were ghetto boys, just like me, Pimp C, Bum B, you can't forget about street military, everybody love them, E.P.M.D, Public Enemy, Eric B. and Rock M, "Yea" that was the oldies, when folks use to drink 40 ounces of O E's, and riding on 30's and voles and gold D's, and old schools, use to call you cool breeze, and on TV, It was a different world, and the Cosby show, Bill and Denise, was lil old freaks, and I didn't even know, what about the Dukes of hazard, Luke and Bo, they should've called that, the Daisy show. You remember Color purple, purple rain, who's the boss, and Growing pains, Happy days and Good times, DAMN! DAMN! DAMN! James, that was the good old days man !

THE CITY OF POETRY

To me, poetry, is like a great city built from love, and new ideas, where there are no fears, and no mistakes, And everybody in it, has what it takes, to conquer their dreams, because they know what it means, to love, They know the passion of a kiss, and the comfort of a hug, This is a place where your words can heal, so you can feel, like you want to feel, And that's what gives you the power, to want to build, your desires, and fulfill your fate, It's A place, where it's never too late, Because you always have time, and a peace of mind, Because whatever you're looking for, it's never that hard to find, Line upon line, the sun seems to shine, What a beautiful design, divine, where every moment, is one of a kind, And every minute is meant, Even though the memories may fade, the time was still spent, Sent from above, and it's something special that this does, That makes you want to fall in love, Just because, To me, poetry, is a city of songs, where the birds seem to sing, all night long, And nothing ever goes wrong, Because love, gives life to your words, so that they can live on, Every paragraph every phrase, brings length to your days, every parable and metaphor, lets you fly, and lets you sore, High above your situations and circumstance, and gives you a second chance, to start all over again, To me, poetry, is a city of dreams, where it seems, that there is nothing you can't do, Just get back up again and pursue, And keep your heart on God, and all your dreams shall come true, IN THE CITY OF POETRY!

MAYBE IT'S A SLOW LEAK

"Man", My money has been funny lately, I haven't been getting any hours on my job, and it seems like my boss hates me, My mom says "that I'm crazy", and my dad says, "Boy you're just lazy, soft like a lady", but maybe just maybe, it's the way that they made me, or how they raised me, I've been spoiled since a baby, anything I wanted they gave me, Now only the love of Jesus can save me, and make me strong where I'm weak, because I know I don't have a flat, maybe it's just a slow leak, But I have to figure out what's going on in my life, Because every time I meet a chick, she ends up being the wrong one, right, or she just the wrong type, I'm not saying they are wrong but they just are not right, Because I don't want just anybody for a wife, I want somebody genuine and real, who feels like I feel, That will fill me up with love, like a home cooked meal, a shelter a shield, that will always help me build, someone that knows how to act, and scratch my back, just a little, See I know where I'm going, and I see where I'm at, But what I'm trying to see, if this is a slow leak or a flat, Because I'm at a place in my life, where I need to find me, and try to see, could this poetry, somehow be my ministry, capturing words, and setting them free, Then all of a sudden I heard a voice telling me, "Son don't you worry I will get you there, Your tires have never went flat, and your slow leak has never needed air!

I'M JUST TAKING IT EASY

I have been thru some rainy days, where it seemed like the rain, just wouldn't go away, and the clouds just kept getting darker, and the day just kept getting harder, But I knew the sun would soon shine, and leave those bad days behind, Now the skies are clear, and has cleared my mind, So I guess this is just my relaxing time, That's why I'm just taking it easy, I might just go sit up under a tree, hide in the shade until the sun decides to find me, Are I might just take a dip in the pool, first tap my toes in the water, to see if it's cool, It's a beautiful day and I don't know what to do, But I have to do something before this day is thru, I was thinking about writing a letter, but the day just keeps getting better, That's why I'm just taking it easy, A friend of mind said, that she might stop by for a while, And I hope that she does, because, I just love to see her smile, Mean while, I'll just play a nice song, Because I can jam good music, all night long, And love songs, take me somewhere safe, sometimes it's hard to leave that special place, Because I fantasize, in my mind sometimes, and I was there living inside those rhymes, That's why I'm just taking it easy, I lift my head up, and it's not a cloud in the sky, And I wonder could it be getting easier as the days go by, so I try to ride the waves of the wind, And enjoy my day, because soon, all good things come to an end, But for now, let us pretend, that, that's not true, while we get lost in the things, that we love to do, Relax and chill, and just feel free, As for me, I'm just taking it easy!

A NEW YEAR

5, 4, 3, 2, 1, Happy New Year, Then I heard a whistle blow, All of a sudden, I looked up and recognized that I was standing up under a mistletoe, And all that passed thru my mind, is where did all the time go, Exactly, evidently, I handled last year badly, But since I'm still here, I won't let this year pass me, It's a new chance for change, and endless possibilities, and an opportunity to rearrange some things, In my life, try to turn my wrongs to rights, reunite, with family and friends, These are the things we think about when our year comes to an end, The decisions that were made, all the games that we played, those were the roads, that we chose to pave, A hole of a grave, in the mist of a maze, somehow has made, us slaves, to our yesterdays, But it doesn't have to be this way, there is a way to be free, It starts somewhere between changing who you are, and finding out who you need to be, Humbleness is the key, and then there is perception, The way you view things can be used as a weapon, If you fall, get up stepping, Don't give the enemy a chance to catch you slipping, use self discipline, Maybe then, you'll listen when, you hear the voice of change, Then things, won't seem so strange when a New Year has came! "HAPPY NEW YEARS"!

IN THE MORNING

You can get a lot done when the city is still, and this is for real, You can almost recognize what you really feel, Just sitting there with your soul in submission, you start to visualize how to put your life in position, And all you have to do is just listen, To the voice that dwells inside, that will provide everything you have been missing, But faith plays the largest part, Because you have to trust in what comes from your heart, This decides if things will be easier or harder, If you pursue righteousness, life will just, fall in order, Then your heavenly father, will lead the way, He will give you more than you deserve, when he hears the words that you pray, So every morning of every day, Get up early so God can hear what you have to say, Ask him to show you the way, invite God in your life and ask him to stay, Do this in the morning, When the world is a sleep, and you have a peace of mind, when it comes to praying, this is the perfect time, Then you can start trying to see what the day is going to bring, putting away all your fears, so that new ideas can start to spring, Then the birds will start to sing, Guiding you, into, a new harmony, That's why I get up early in the morning, because the morning sets me free, By leaving my Yesterday's behind, and leading me where I need to be, Focus, and taking notice of what God has for me, Passionately pursuing a new day, with a positive state of mind, Eyes open wide, as I look up to the skies, Thank God I'm alive, It's morning time!

I KNOW IT'S REAL

What lies ahead of me, I can only imagine, I know that it's real cause I can feel the compassion, but still patiently waiting for something to happen, while I'm trapped in, this lonely old soul, just trying to figure out which way I should go, should I shine in the sun, Are just freeze in the snow, I saw a shadow of salvation, in a cracked open door, a large ray of light, that made me fall to the floor, an angel in white, with a radiant glow, I hung my head down low, to humble myself on my knees, and I tried to take heed, to what he was telling me, then suddenly, I heard, son you are free, you've been waiting patiently, and I see you hearken to me, now arise, open your eyes, so you can walk into victory, then I arose, and I saw the doors opened up wide, he said son this is yours go ahead and walk inside, you are the groom, and this is your bride, the most beautiful sight that I have ever seen, then I woke up in chills, could this have all been a dream, but you would have thought this was real, if you would have saw, what I seen!

THAT'S MOMMA'S LIL MAN

Since I was a child you had a lot of faith in me, when we would be at the park, you would always just let me run free, you were never afraid that anything would happen to me, you would be like, that's momma's lil man, and that always encouraged me to be, all that I could be, and that let me see that I can, and made me one hell of a man, now I understand what your faith did, and it's helping me now that I have kids, but it seems like these days, raising kids or harder, that even had me thinking that I wasn't a good father, my temper kept getting shorter and shorter, tell I sort of, caught on to the whole parenting thing, what I found out was kids play games, so I knew I had to start playing games too, and Momma it's funny how I started reminding myself of you, but I guess when there lil men, you have to let a lil man do, what lil men do, so momma your lil man just wants to thank you!

Chapter SIX

"Quotes"

QUOTES! Whenever you find yourself doubting how far you can go. Just remember how far you have come. Remember everything you have faced, all the battles you have won. And all the fears you have overcome. UNKNOWN AUTHOR!

Always stay true to yourself because there are very few people who will always be true to you! Unknown Author:

Everyone makes mistakes in life that doesn't mean they have to pay for them for the rest of their life. Sometimes good people make bad choices, that doesn't mean they are bad, it means they are human! Unknown Author!

Some changes happen so deep down inside, that only you know about them. Not sure of the Author!

Simple minds talk about people, Average minds talk about events, Great minds talk about ideas, Not sure of this Author!

Never lower your standards to be in someone's presence, Make them raise their standards to be in your presence, Author, Royal Shepherd!

There is no elevator to success, you must climb the stairs, Author Unknown!

Inner peace begins the moment you choose not to allow another person or event to control your emotions, Author Unknown!

QUOTES! There is no passion to be found, in settling for a life that is less than the one you are capable of living, Nelson Mandela!

Never be afraid to fall apart, because it's an opportunity to rebuild yourself the way you wish you had been all along! Author Unknown!

At any giving moment you have the power to say, This is not how my story is going to end, Author Unknown!

You know my name, not my story, You have heard of what I've done not what I have been thru! Author Unknown!

THE BREAD THEORY, If your friends only have crumbs, if you're in need it's only possible for them to give you crumbs, But if you just know, Someone with loaves, at your least it's possible for you to get an end bread, Author: Royal Shepherd!

Don't pay attention to the ground, when someone is trying to show you the skies, Author Royal Shepherd!

Why worry about what's right in front of you, when it's so many better things ahead of you, Royal Shepherd!

Sometimes love can make you feel like all your dreams can come true. And sometimes love can make your dreams seem like a nightmare to you. Author: Royal Shepherd!

We have to believe that people can change, Cause if we don't, that makes it impossible for us to change! Author: Royal Shepherd!

Struggling is just a circumstance or a situation that you have to make a choice or decision to get out of, or to just let go of! Author: Royal Shepherd!

Tell the truth, to give people an option to make their own decisions! Author: Royal Shepherd!

QUOTES: Here's to the crazy ones, the misfits, the rebels the trouble makers the round pegs in the square holes, The ones who see things differently - there not fond of rules, you can quote them, disagree with them, glorify or vilify them, But the only thing you can't do, is ignore them, because they change things, they push the human race forward, And while some may see them as the crazy ones, we see genius, Because the ones who are crazy enough to think that they can change the world, Are the ones who do! Author: Steve Jobs

Your time is limited, so don't waste it living someone else's life, Don't be trapped by Dogma - Which is living with the results of other people's thinking, Don't let the noise of other's opinions, drown out your own inner voice, And most important, have the courage to follow your own heart and intuition, Because they somehow already

---

POET TREE IN MOTION   ROYAL SHEPHERD

know, what you truly want to become, everything else is secondary: Author: Steve Jobs

QUOTES: If you don't want anybody to rain on your parade. Don't let them know what street it's on! Author: Pastor Rudy Rasmus

To be yourself, in a world that's constantly changing you into something you're not, or making you into something else, Being your greatest accomplishment! Author: Ralph Waldo Emerson!

Go confidently in the direction of your dreams, And you will live the life you always imagined! Author: Henry David Thoreau !

Wanting something is not the same thing as going after it: Miss Dubose!

The ones that angers you is the one who controls you, Don't ever give anyone that much power, Especially the ones who do it intentionally! Author: Unknown

Never waste your time explaining who you are to people who are committed to misunderstanding you! Author: Unknown:

Never let your circumstances or situation, Keep you from accomplishing what you know in your heart you were meant to accomplish! Author: Royal Shepherd!

All though the memories may fade, The time was still spent! Author: Royal Shepherd

QUOTES: It's never to late, to become who you might have been! Author: George Elliot

What lies before us and behind us are tiny matters compared to what lies within us! Author: Walt Emerson

Great spirits have always encountered violent opposition from mediocre minds! Author: Albert Einstein

There are two primary choices in life, to accept conditions as they are, Or accepting the responsibility for changing them! Author: Dennis Waitley

Don't let what you can not do, interfere with what you can do! Author: John Wooden

No individual rain drop considers itself responsible for the whole flood! Author: Unknown

When writing the story of your life, Don't let anyone else hold the pen! Author: Unknown

We have to start being real with ourselves and stop pretending. And maybe just maybe then, we will have a happy ending! Author: Royal Shepherd

QUOTES: The truth establishes a relationship, Because if you loose the trust, you damage the heart, if you damage the heart, You kill the love! Author: Royal Shepherd!

Love is when people care about you, through action and time, not sex or attraction, But each person gets to choose, so choose correctly, choose someone, who chooses to love you! Author: Royal Shepherd!

The reason it's so hard to trust people, Because it's so many good people, with bad intentions! Author: Royal Shepherd!

There is more honor, when an enemy is honest, about their hate towards you, Then for a friend to lie, about the love, that they have for you! Author: Royal Shepherd!

True success doesn't come from knowing who you are, It comes from knowing who you may become! Author: Royal Shepherd!

If you always remember the hardest trial you ever faced in your life, It makes it easier to handle future adversities! Author: Royal Shepherd!

You can't do anything, about anything, you can't do anything about! Author: Royal Shepherd!

People with money, brag about how much money they spent, People without money brag about how much money they save! Author: Royal Shepherd

Special Shout Outs to:

"God" Who made this all possible!

Gwendolyn Hebert[*]: For the love and the life you've giving me, without you none of this would be possible!

Louella William And Family: Thank you Aunt Lou for all the love and support

Kristopher T Gray[†]: You are my inspiration, and the best part of me is you!

Brittany Righteous B. Hebert[‡]: Thanks for the love you are truly one of A kind, Love you B.!

Kalub Doyle JR[§]: Your faith in me has been the wing beneath my wing!

Josette T. and Jules T. Hebert[**]: Can't forget about Y'all love you!

Felton White[††]: From For life entertainment: You were God sent. Thank you for everything "ONE"

Marcus The Author Henry: Thanks for you guidance, time and inspiration, God bless you Bro!

Shon Shine: Thanks a lot For all the encouragement and help that you gave me getting this project completed!

---

[*] *My mother*

[†] *My son*

[‡] *My Niece*

[§] *My big brother*

[**] *My sister and nephew*

[††] *My brother: From another mother*

Allen Butler: True friend indeed, May God always be your guide. Love You Bro!

Thomas Anderson Jr: Thanks lil cuz for always believing in me!

Varion and Perniece Howard love you both sincerely with all my heart!

- Anderson Family
- Hébert Family
- Sinegal Family
- Pierre August Family
- Fisher Family
- Arceneaux Family
- Saint John downtown Family
- Gray Family
- McCardell Family
- McCray Family
- Battle Family
- Demochett Family
- McZeal Family

About The Author

Royal Shepherd Was born down south in a small town in 1975 with a humble upbringing, with the help of my mother Gwendolyn Sinegal. Then I moved up north to a smaller town with my grandparents Maggie and Stanford Anderson for a few years, In those few years I found a passion for nature. And learned a lot of values, that I still possess today. By the grace of God, I was able to notice that I was different, and I had a purpose in life, that would lead me to open the eyes of the lost, and to strengthen the weak, inspire the youth, and to encourage the less fortunate to have confidence in their selves and faith in God. All in all, that's what made me Royal! I am, "The Royal Shepherd"

Inspirational Songs

I'm Gonna Make It If I Try

I'm Gonna make it if I try, I've been thru it, and that's no lie, but I get better and I got by, I'm Gonna make it yea!

   I'm sitting at the mountain top, trying to get this old message out, That I've been high and I've been low, sometimes I had no place to go, but I kept searching for a better way, on my knees every night I pray. That if I keep my faith I'll get it, if it's about the good lord I'm with it, I'm Gonna make it, yea.

   I'm Gonna make it if I try, I've been thru it, and that's no lie, but I get better and I got by, I'm Gonna make it yea.

       I've been in there and I've been out, I know Y'all know what I'm talking about, sometimes I get weary, but I don't worry, because my testimony, will tell his story, that's why I use my prayers as a weapon, so if I fall, I'll get up stepping, now everyday it feels like heaven, I'm Gonna make it yea.

I'm Gonna make it if I try, I've been thru it, and that's no lie, but I get better and I got by, I'm Gonna make it yea.

I've been battered and I've been bruised, talked about and I've been misused, I may win some, and I may loose, down and out, but I'm not confused, about my faith, and I just can't fake it, I've been thru it but I can take it, they can bend it, but they can't break it, that's why, I'm Gonna make it.

POET TREE IN MOTION   ROYAL SHEPHERD

I'm Gonna make it if I try, I've been thru it, and that's no lie, but I get better and I got by, I'm Gonna make it yea!

Written By: The Royal Shepherd

www.ingramcontent.com/pod-product-compliance
Lightning Source LLC
Chambersburg PA
CBHW021848220426
43663CB00005B/444